SUPER SHEROES OF HISTORY

Global Activists

Women Who Made a Difference

DEVRA NEWBERGER SPEREGEN

Children's Press®
An imprint of Scholastic Inc.

Thank you to Brittany Schulman for her insights into Indigenous Peoples' history and culture.

Picture credits:
Photos ©: cover top: Goldman Environmental Prize; cover center top: Marcelo Correia/Camera Press/Redux; cover center bottom: Radu Sigheti/Reuters/Alamy Images; cover bottom: CARL-JOHAN UTSI/TT News Agency/AFP/Getty Images; 5 left: Goldman Environmental Prize; 5 center left: Marcelo Correia/Camera Press/Redux; 5 center right: Radu Sigheti/Reuters/Alamy Images; 5 right: CARL-JOHAN UTSI/TT News Agency/AFP/Getty Images; 6 left: Radu Sigheti/Reuters/Alamy Images; 7 top right: EvaRijnkels/Getty Images; 8 top: Karel Prinsloo/AP Images; 8 bottom: John McConnico/AP Images; 9 bottom: James Wakibia/SOPA Images/LightRocket/Getty Images; 10 top: Jake Lyell/Alamy Images; 11 center: Laurent Zabulon/Gamma-Rapho/Getty Images; 12 top: ton koene/Alamy Images; 14 top: Toby Melville/Reuters/Alamy Images; 15 top: Angelo Cozzi/Archivio Angelo Cozzi/Mondadori/Getty Images; 15 bottom: Universal History Archive/UIG/Shutterstock; 16 bottom: Mast Irham/EPA/Shutterstock; 17 top: COLE WILSON/The New York Times/Redux; 18 top: Wiktor Dabkowski/dpa picture alliance/Alamy Images; 19 top: Steve Rhodes/Flickr; 20 bottom: Morteza Nikoubazl/Reuters/Alamy Images; 21 top: eFesenko/Alamy Images; 22 top: Marcelo Correia/Camera Press/Redux; 24 top: Owais Aslam Ali/Asianet-Pakistan/Alamy Images; 25 top: PictureLux/The Hollywood Archive/Alamy Images; 25 bottom: Jamal Saidi/Reuters/Alamy Images; 26 top right: Nigel Waldron/Getty Images; 27 center: Irfan/Xinhua/Alamy Images; 28 top: CARL-JOHAN UTSI/TT News Agency/AFP/Getty Images; 31 top background: Chris J Ratcliffe/Getty Images; 31 top foreground: Alexandros Michailidis/Alamy Images; 31 bottom: Tomwsulcer/Wikipedia; 32 top: Finnbarr Webster/Getty Images; 33 top: Guglielmo Mangiapane/Reuters/Alamy Images; 36 top: Tim Graham/Getty Images; 37 top: Thomas D Mcavoy/The LIFE Picture Collection/Shutterstock; 37 bottom: Alexandre Meneghini/Reuters/Alamy Images; 38 top: Everett/Shutterstock; 39 top: Goldman Environmental Prize; 40 bottom: Allison Carden Hanes/One Health Productions; 41 top: Jacquelyn Martin/AP Images; 42 top right: Luiz Rampelotto/EuropaNewswire/dpa picture alliance/Alamy Images; 42 bottom left: Kyodo News/Newscom; 42 bottom right: Toby Melville/Reuters/Alamy Images; 43 top left: UNEP/Flickr; 43 bottom center: ZUMA Press, Inc./Alamy Images; 44-45: pop_jop/Getty Images.

All other photos © Shutterstock.

Library of Congress Cataloging-in-Publication Data Available

ISBN 978-1-338-84065-0 (library binding) | ISBN 978-1-338-84066-7 (paperback)

10 9 8 7 6 5 4 3 2 1   23 24 25 26 27

Printed in China   62
First edition, 2023

Series produced for Scholastic by Parcel Yard Press

Contents

Who Are the Super SHEroes of History?

Throughout history, women have ruled countries, led soldiers into battle, changed laws, come up with new ways of thinking, and worked to improve life for everyone. Women's actions and ideas have changed the course of history for whole societies, whole countries, and even the whole world. Women have made a difference. Often, however, their achievements have gone unrecognized.

This book celebrates the life and accomplishments of twelve of these women, twelve Super SHEroes of History! They are all global activists who have worked and are working for a better world for everyone.

Global activists are people who organize protests and campaigns that ask governments and companies around the world to act in fairer ways.

SUPER SHEROES OF HISTORY

Berta Cáceres

Malala Yousafzai

Wangari Maathai

Greta Thunberg

The Super SHEroes in this book have worked to make the world a better place. They have taken action to protect nature and the environment, tried to ensure that everyone gets a good education, and looked after the poor and sick. They all had to overcome many obstacles but succeeded in making a difference to the times in which they lived.

This book brings the stories of these Super SHEroes to you! And while you read them, remember:

Your story can make a difference, too. You can become a Super SHEro of History!

Wangari Maathai

Wangari started the Green Belt Movement in Africa, a project that paid poor women to plant trees in the countryside. Her activism restored natural habitats and improved conditions for the poorest people.

SUPER SHEROES OF HISTORY

Wangari grew up in Nyeri, a rural community in Kenya. She left Africa to study biology in the United States and Germany. Then, Wangari came back to Kenya to get her doctorate degree. In 1971, she became the first woman in all of East and Central Africa to earn a **PhD**.

datafile

Born: April 1, 1940

Died: September 25, 2011

Place of birth: Nyeri, Kenya

Role: Environmentalist

Super SHEro for: Being the founder of the Green Belt Movement and becoming the first African woman to win the Nobel Peace Prize

Wangari grew concerned as she saw that her once lush, green homeland was steadily being destroyed by **deforestation**. There were shortages of food and clean water. Freshwater streams had been left to dry up, too, and wildlife was quickly disappearing.

This is Mount Kenya, the highest peak in Kenya. Wangari grew up in the highland countryside nearby.

Women in **rural** communities like Nyeri were suffering. They were forced to walk for hours to fetch water and firewood, and they struggled to provide for their families. So Wangari developed a way to improve the environment and also help women: plant trees!

Fifteen million Kenyans do not have access to safe, clean drinking water.

Wangari set up an organization called the Green Belt Movement (GBM) in 1977. It called upon poor, rural women to help slow deforestation and stop soil **erosion**.

The GBM trained whole communities of women to grow seedlings and plant saplings in rows to form "green belts" of trees. It educated them on the proper ways to collect and store rainwater. Millions of new trees were soon planted across Kenya, and whole villages became green again. Wangari was praised for her efforts and became known as Mama Miti, **Swahili** for Mother of Trees.

Wangari planted many trees herself all over Africa.

Did You Know?

Wangari won the Nobel Peace Prize in 2004 for her contribution to green development and democracy. She was the first African woman ever to win this important prize. She once said: "When we plant trees, we plant the seeds of peace and seeds of hope. We also secure the future for our children."

The new trees did more than just turn Kenya green again. Wangari's GBM provided much needed money for some of the poorest women in Kenya. Many of the GBM workers could not read or write, but the paid work helped improve their lives and boosted their self-esteem.

As more and more rural communities flourished in Kenya, Wangari and other leaders of the GBM created the Pan African Green Belt Network in 1986. It brought community-based tree planting to other African countries.

New trees are being planted in Kenya's natural forests.

Wangari thought that another good way to stop **poverty** and hunger in Africa was to stop governments from borrowing large sums of money from foreign banks. She thought the money used to pay back the banks could be spent in better ways.

The borrowed money was often used to build expensive skyscrapers. Wangari started with a protest against Kenya's president, who was planning to build the tallest building in Africa for use as government offices. The project was going to cost $200 million, and it would mean destroying a large, popular park used by Nairobi's poorest citizens.

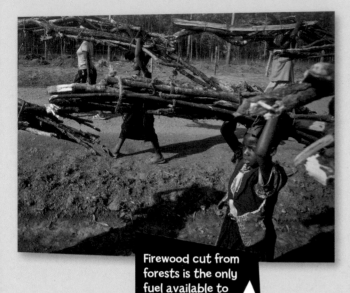

Firewood cut from forests is the only fuel available to many Kenyans.

Thanks to Wangari, Kenyans still enjoy the open space of Uhuru Park in downtown Nairobi.

"People are starving, they need food, they need medicine and they need education," Wangari protested. "They do not need a skyscraper." Her protest was successful and the skyscraper project was canceled.

In 2002, Wangari was elected to Kenya's **parliament** and became Assistant Minister for Environment. Wangari made speeches at the United Nations spreading her ideas about preserving the environment. **When she died in 2011, Wangari was recognized around the world as a leading environmental activist and peacemaker.**

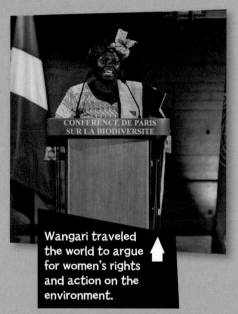

Wangari traveled the world to argue for women's rights and action on the environment.

What Would You Do?

Wangari noticed that the deforestation of Africa was causing hunger and poverty.

If your community faced a big problem such as hunger or poverty, what would you do about it?

Wangari grew up in the Kenyan countryside. She lived in a very simple house that did not have running water or electricity. In the 1950s, Kenyan girls were expected to help a lot more around the house than the boys.

Wangari took notice early on of the role women played in the home. Wangari's father was the head of the house and made all the decisions. Her mother had no say in family matters but did most of the physical housework, like fetching water and gathering firewood.

Most farmworkers, such as this tea picker, were women.

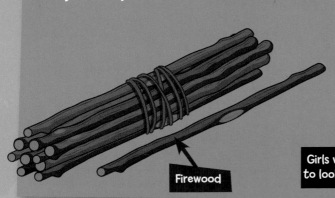

Firewood

Girls were taught how to look after the home.

12

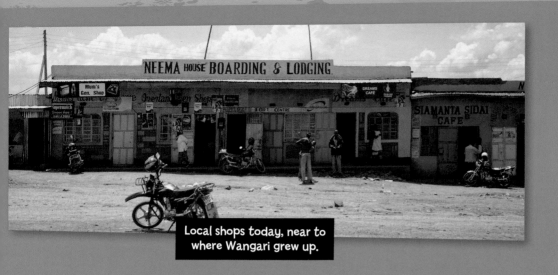

Local shops today, near to where Wangari grew up.

Kenyan women and girls were not encouraged to get an education back then, either. (Wangari was exceptionally smart, and her older brother convinced their parents to send her to boarding school.) At the time, Kenya was fighting for independence from Britain. At her boarding school, Wangari was protected from the violence of the struggle. She did so well at school that she earned a scholarship to attend college in the United States.

Masih Alinejad

Masih is a journalist who was forced into **exile** from Iran for speaking out against its **oppressive** government. From her home in the United States, Masih fights for human rights, even though it puts her life in danger.

datafile

Born: September 11, 1976

Place of Birth: Qomi Kola, Iran

Role: Journalist and campaigner

Super SHEro for: Creating the My Stealthy Freedom campaign online. This gave Iranian women a place to share their unhappiness about Iran's clothing rules.

Growing up in a strict Muslim family in a small village in northern Iran, Masih was known as a *shahr-ashoob,* or "troublemaker." She was always speaking out, challenging authority and complaining about all the things girls were not permitted to do in Iran: No sitting next to boys in school, no riding bikes in public, and no swimming if boys were around. Masih thought the laws in Iran were unfair to women and girls.

Masih was two in 1979, when the king of Iran was forced out of power, and the stricter **Ayatollah** Khomeini took over.

Life changed drastically for Iranians, but especially for women. They no longer could dress how they wanted or go anywhere without a male **chaperone**. They couldn't go to the beach or the theater. And whenever they left the house, they were ordered to wear a **hijab** to cover their hair and a **chador** over their clothes. Special police patrolled the streets to enforce the Ayatollah's rules. Women who were uncovered in public were fined or sent to prison.

A mural of Ayatollah Khomeini. His picture is seen all over Iran.

In 1979, the Iranian people rose up against the king (left) and his government.

Schoolgirls were ordered to wear a hijab, too. Masih wore hers everywhere, around friends and family, and even to sleep. She was unhappy. She yearned for the same freedoms enjoyed by boys.

In high school, Masih was still a troublemaker. She refused to wear her chador one day, and her father didn't speak to her for two months. She spoke out against the government and got arrested and spent a month in prison for handing out pamphlets calling for freedom. In her twenties Masih became a journalist, but got banned from reporting after an article

Masih got in trouble by saying that Mahmoud Ahmadinejad, Iran's president at the time, was only supported by people to whom he had paid money.

she wrote exposed government **corruption.** She was then suspended for wearing red shoes to work.

The Iranian authorities harassed her and tried to get her fired from her newspaper job. They spread lies about her and her family. The abuse got so bad that Masih felt she was in danger of being arrested again. She fled Iran and moved to the United Kingdom.

Masih was forced to build a new life outside of Iran. ⬆

Did You Know?

Muslim women wear a hijab for many reasons. Some see it as a sign of passage into adulthood. To others it shows cultural pride or family tradition. Masih believes women should have freedom of choice and decide for themselves whether to wear it or not.

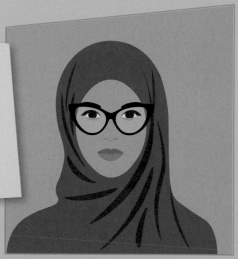

Masih has discussed clothing bans across the world.

In May 2014, while living in London, Masih posted old photos of herself on Facebook without her hijab. She wrote about how in Iran that simple act would be illegal. Thousands of Iranian women replied with messages that contained photos and videos of themselves without a hijab. Masih started a Facebook page called My Stealthy Freedom. It soon had many thousands of followers who posted their own photos.

Masih says that the people who post on My Stealthy Freedom are not activists. Instead, they are ordinary women speaking out. The movement angers the Iranian authorities, who have made trouble for Masih's family back home.

Masih now lives in New York, and in 2021 an attempt to kidnap her there and take her to Iran was stopped by the police. **Even though she is in danger, Masih continues to support the rights of Muslim women around the world.**

Masih often appears in public to talk about her campaign.

What Would You Do?

Masih was mad that her brother could come and go from the house but she had to stay at home. Girls were expected to stay indoors and out of sight.

What do you do when you feel the rules are too strict?

What would you have done if you were Masih?

Life in the Times of Masih Alinejad

IRAN: 2000s

When Iranian people are in public they must follow many rules. If they break the rules, people can get in trouble with the police. However, Iranians still manage to have fun and enjoy life.

Tehran is Iran's capital city.

Iran's women's volleyball team is world class.

Both women and men are required to wear modest clothes that do not show off or attract attention. For women this means covering up completely, especially by using a hijab so their hair is not showing. There are rules for men, too. Tight pants, shorts, short-sleeved shirts, and sleeveless shirts are not allowed in public. Men are forbidden to grow long hair.

Inside a *zurkhaneh* in Tehran.

Iranians love watching soccer. The men go to the stadium, but women generally watch from home. Top sports in Iran include wrestling and volleyball. Iran is home to *zurkhaneh*. These are meeting places similar to gyms—the name means "house of strength." They are used for sports and performances. The idea for *zurkhaneh* dates back thousands of years. In the past these places were only for men. However, more and more Iranian women are now using them as well.

Wrestling

Hijab

In Iran, girls must wear a hijab in public from the age of nine.

21

Malala Yousafzai

SUPER SHEROES OF HISTORY

When **extremists** banned girls in her city from going to school, young Malala spoke out. She was nearly killed for it. But she survived and became a voice for female education and the world's youngest Nobel Peace Prize winner.

Malala lived in Mingora, in the Swat region of Pakistan. She went to a school set up by her father, who is a teacher. When **Taliban** extremists took control of Swat in 2007, they banned many things, like television and music. They punished those who refused to obey orders. In 2008, the Taliban banned girls from going to school.

datafile

Born: July 12, 1997

Place of birth: Mingora, Pakistan

Role: Education campaigner

Super SHEro for: Taking on the Taliban in Pakistan and becoming the youngest winner of the Nobel Peace Prize

Malala grew up in Mingora, in the mountains of northern Pakistan.

Malala was eleven. She couldn't imagine a life without school. One day her father took her to speak to some journalists. She gave a speech, asking, "How dare the Taliban take away my right to an education?"

Malala's message spread across Pakistan. She started writing on a popular **Urdu** news website (using a fake name). She wrote about the terrible living conditions under Taliban rule. She described how they had blown up schools and executed Pakistanis who didn't follow their rules.

Girls and women across Pakistan showed their support for Malala after she was shot.

Malala wrote that she wanted to speak out publicly on behalf of girls about their right to learn. This made her a target. Even though the Taliban had lost control of Swat in 2009, the extremists still saw Malala as an enemy. On October 9, 2012, fifteen-year-old Malala was riding a bus with her friends, when a masked gunman got on and demanded, "Who is Malala?" Then he shot her in the head.

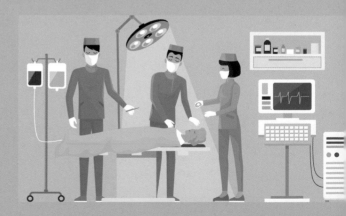

Malala was rushed to the hospital and was not expected to survive. Surgeons had to remove part of her skull to relieve swelling in her brain. She woke up ten days later in a hospital in England and did not even remember the attack. Doctors had to tell her what happened, and how people all over the world were thinking of her.

Malala took to the world stage at the United Nations.

Malala recovered and did not suffer brain damage. Five months later, she started at a new school in England. That summer, on her sixteenth birthday, Malala was well enough to speak at the United Nations. Malala told her story to world leaders, then demanded their governments provide girls with an education.

Did You Know?

Malala created the Malala Fund to ensure that girls around the world receive twelve years of free, safe, high-quality education. By the time she was eighteen she had raised enough money to open a school for girls in Syria. On behalf of the world's children, she demanded that leaders "invest in books instead of bullets."

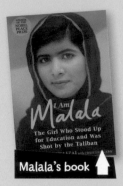

Malala's book

One year after the attack, Malala published her autobiography, *I Am Malala: The Girl Who Stood Up for Education and Was Shot by the Taliban*. A version for younger kids came out in 2018 called *My Story of Standing Up for Girls' Rights*. In October 2014, Malala won the Nobel Peace Prize in recognition of her work with the Malala Fund. At seventeen, she was the youngest person ever to receive the award.

Malala has finished her education now. She travels the world, often to places damaged by wars, asking for girls to be educated in the same way as boys.

Malala shows off her Nobel Peace Prize in 2014.

What Would You Do?

Though she was nearly killed, Malala believes she did the right thing by standing up to the Taliban.

What would you do if your town or neighborhood was taken over by extremists?

Would you speak out, even if it was dangerous?

STOP THE HATE

Life in the Times of Malala Yousafzai
PAKISTAN: 2000s

The Swat Valley, where Malala lived, was once a popular tourist spot in Pakistan known for its summer festivals and beautiful sunsets. Then the Taliban took over in 2007 and everything changed. Women could no longer dress how they wanted, visit stores, dance, or go to parties.

In the countryside girls are still often taught separately from boys.

Men were prohibited from shaving their beards. If people disobeyed Taliban rules, they were killed. Malala hid her books under her shawl and walked to school every day in fear of the Taliban.

The Swat Valley is a beautiful region.

In 2008, the Taliban ordered all girls' schools to close, including Malala's. The Taliban lost power in 2009. Pakistani girls are once again allowed to go to school. However, even today in poor, rural areas, only about 8 percent of girls learn to read.

Greta Thunberg

Greta is the world's leading climate activist. When she was only fifteen, Greta became famous by refusing to go to school until the government in Sweden, her home country, did something to stop **climate change**. She has since taken this fight around the world.

SUPER SHEROES OF HISTORY

datafile

When Greta was eight, she watched a film in class about climate change and its harmful effects on the planet. She saw starving polar bears and plastic garbage floating in the ocean. She cried. Greta's classmates seemed concerned, too. But when the film was over, they went back to talking and thinking about other things. Greta couldn't do that. The pictures from the movie got stuck in her head.

Born: January 3, 2003

Place of birth: Stockholm, Sweden

Role: Climate activist

Super SHEro for: Inspiring young people around the world to fight climate change

Greta became more and more depressed about climate change. She was shocked that adults weren't doing enough to stop it. She was so upset, she stopped speaking and eating.

Greta was diagnosed with Asperger's syndrome. This condition can cause people to concentrate on a single interest. "I overthink," she says about herself. "Some people can just let things go, but I can't, especially if there's something that worries me or makes me sad."

Greta's school strike inspired children to hold climate rallies around the world.

At fifteen, Greta thought hard about the problems caused by climate change, such as droughts, melting glaciers, and rising sea levels. She made life changes to avoid contributing to the problem. She became vegetarian and refused to eat animal-based foods because they contribute to climate change. She stopped flying, because airplanes damage the environment.

In August 2018, there were devastating heat waves and wildfires in Sweden. Greta skipped school to strike outside the Swedish parliament building. She held a big sign that read "Skolstrejk för Klimatet," which in English means "School Strike for Climate."

SYSTEM CHANGE
NOT CLIMATE CHANGE!

Climate change is making the ice melt in the Arctic and Antarctic regions.

Teens around the world held their own school strikes to support Greta.

SKOLSTREJK FÖR KLIMATET

Greta made the news, and the following week a few people joined her. Many more children went on strike as word of Greta's protest spread. The protest caught the attention of the international press. Soon tens of thousands of students around the world were skipping school to take part in Greta's climate strikes, known on social media as #FridaysforFuture.

Did You Know?

Greta's school strike was inspired by teen activists in Florida who were protesting to end gun violence. After a mass shooting at their school, the teens held school walkouts. They also organized the March For Our Lives, which inspired hundreds of thousands of protesters to march through American cities.

In 2019, Greta sailed to New York City to address world leaders at the United Nations Climate Action Summit. She demanded that world leaders listen to scientists' warnings about climate change. She was angry that people in power had not taken action for many years. "How dare you?" she asked. In 2021, she again called for immediate action at an event in Milan, Italy. "Thirty years of blah, blah, blah," she said of all the promises to stop **global warming**. "And where has this led us?"

Greta sailed to New York, because flying would damage the climate.

Climate activists in Kolkata, India, hold a sign inspired by Greta's speech.

Greta has become the face of the global fight against climate change. She says her Asperger's is a "superpower" that helps her continue her fight. She describes her movement as a wave of change. It has caught the attention of millions of people—mostly teenagers—around the globe. **Greta's impact on our approach to climate change clearly shows how one person can change the world!**

Greta still appears at meetings around the world to urge governments to act on climate change.

What Would You Do?

Greta has inspired climate marches all over the world to bring awareness to climate change and its affect on our planet.

Would you take part in a climate march?

How do you think your parents would feel if you did?

Life in the Times of Greta Thunberg

THE PLANET: 2020s

Greta has made it clear that we all need to start protecting the planet. Plastic pollution is clogging our oceans and destroying sea life, yet we continue to buy bottled water. Fuel emissions put our climate in danger, but still we rely on non-electric cars.

The world's weather is becoming more extreme.

In 2018, a United Nations report explained that if the whole world did not stop releasing greenhouse gases such as carbon dioxide into the atmosphere, the global average temperature would rise to dangerous levels. As the world heated up, we would likely see more extreme weather.

Devastating heat waves, droughts, and intense storms, such as hurricanes, have become more common across the world. If this continues, then some places in the world will be too hot or too wet to live in. Some animals and plants may become extinct. But Greta's mission to get the world to act is working because more people—especially children—are taking the threats from climate change seriously.

There are many things we can do every day to help our planet. We can try to walk and cycle instead of driving. We can reduce what we buy, reuse things instead of throwing them away, and recycle everything we use. These actions will release less carbon dioxide into the atmosphere, slowing climate change.

Climate change is damaging the habitat of polar bears.

SUPER SHEROES OF HISTORY

Global
Activists
MISSIONARY

Mother Teresa

Mother Teresa was a Catholic nun and **missionary** whose compassion and service brought relief to people who were very poor. Born Agnes Gonxha Bojaxhiu in Macedonia in 1910, she learned to care for the sick and poor from her mother. At eighteen, she moved to Ireland to become a nun, changing her name to Teresa. Teresa was sent to Kolkata, India, to teach at a girls' school. There she witnessed extreme suffering and poverty in the **slums**. She created the Missionaries of Charity to build schools and health clinics in the poorest neighborhoods of the city. In 1979, Mother Teresa won the Nobel Peace Prize for her efforts to reduce human suffering. In 2016, long after her death, Pope Francis made her Saint Teresa of Kolkata.

Mother Teresa
(Macedonia, 1910-1997)

Althea Gibson

Althea Gibson was a pioneer in professional tennis, winning the world's biggest competitions in the 1950s. She became a global goodwill ambassador for the US State Department and gave tennis clinics around the world. After retiring, Althea organized ways for underprivileged city kids to play tennis and other sports. She broke racial barriers and was the first Black woman to appear on the cover of *Sports Illustrated* and *Time* magazine.

Althea Gibson
(United States, 1927-2003)

Maria Grazia Giammarinaro

Maria Grazia Giammarinaro
(Italy, born 1953)

Maria Grazia Giammarinaro is a retired judge from Italy. In 2001, she became famous in Rome for jailing criminals involved in human trafficking. Human traffickers illegally buy and sell people. Maria is working with governments across Europe to stop these criminal gangs.

Global
Activists
EDUCATION CAMPAIGNER

Michelle Obama

Michelle Obama
(United States, born 1964)

"An educated girl can lift up her family, her community, and her country," says former First Lady Michelle Obama. That's why she launched the Global Girls Alliance (GGA) on the International Day of the Girl in 2018. The program, part of the Obama Foundation Michelle created with her husband, former president Barack Obama, works to empower girls around the world through education. Education allows people to support themselves and help others in their neighborhoods. Information collected in 2022 shows that across the world there are still 129 million girls who don't go to school. With the GGA, and some help from communities, Michelle hopes to bring that number down a lot.

Berta Cáceres

Berta Cáceres
(Honduras, 1971–2016)

Berta Cáceres, a member of the Lenca people of Honduras, grew up in the 1980s. It was a violent time across Central America. Berta's mother took in and cared for **refugees** driven from their homes by fighting. Berta learned the value of standing up for people in need.

At college, Berta became an environmental activist for the Lenca community. When a new dam threatened to flood their land and make it harder to collect food and other materials from the forest, Berta led a protest. She managed to stop the dam from being built, but she paid the ultimate price for her actions. In 2016, gunmen working for the dam company broke into her home and killed her.

Global
Activists
WOMEN'S RIGHTS CAMPAIGNER

Emma Watson

Off-screen, the famous *Harry Potter* actress is an activist for women's rights. In 2014, she was appointed a United Nations Goodwill Ambassador for Women and helped launch the HeForShe campaign. This campaign asks men and boys across the world to think more about gender inequality.

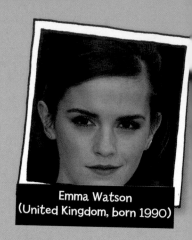

Emma Watson
(United Kingdom, born 1990)

Helena Gualinga

Helena Gualinga
(Ecuador, born 2002)

A member of the Kichwa Sarayaku Indigenous community, Helena grew up in a rain forest threatened by oil companies. Some oil companies destroy nature by building wells and refineries. Helena is a teen activist who stands up to them. In 2020, she helped found the Polluters Out environmental movement. Helena says that her work is about her home, her people, and her family.

Global
Activists
ENVIRONMENTALIST

Isra Hirsi

Young activist Isra Hirsi says the future is created by the conversations and actions that are taking place right now. An environmental justice organizer, Black Lives Matter activist, TikTok star, and college student from Minneapolis, Minnesota, Isra cofounded the US Youth Climate Strike in 2019. She helped organize more than 100,000 young people to strike for climate justice. Driven by her identity as a Black Muslim woman and a child of immigrants (her mother is US representative Ilhan Omar), Isra cares deeply for many issues that impact her family and community.

Isra Hirsi
(United States, born 2003)

#BLACKLIVESMATTER

Timeline

SUPER SHEROES OF HISTORY

Here are some highlights in the lives of Super SHEro activists.

Tennis champ Althea Gibson starts to promote sports to children living in poor neighborhoods.

Mother Teresa wins the Nobel Peace Prize.

Malala Yousafzai is attacked by the Pakistan Taliban.

Emma Watson is appointed a United Nations Goodwill Ambassador.

1972	1977	1979	2001	2012	2014

Wangari Maathai establishes the Green Belt Movement.

Maria Grazia Giammarinaro becomes a judge in Rome, Italy, dealing with serious crimes.

Masih Alinejad starts the My Stealthy Freedom movement.

Berta Cáceres is assassinated for opposing a new dam.

Isra Hirsi cofounds the US Youth Climate Strike.

Kamala Harris becomes the first female US Vice President.

2015 | **2016** | **2018** | **2019** | **2020** | **2021**

The world's governments agree on a plan to combat climate change in Paris, France.

Michelle Obama launches the Global Girls Alliance.

Helena Gualinga helps start the Polluters Out movement.

Greta Thunberg is invited to speak at the Youth4Climate Summit in Italy.

Where in the World?

1. Masih Alinejad
Tehran, Iran
Masih Alinejad uncovered government corruption in Iran's capital city.

2. Berta Cáceres
La Esperanza, Honduras
Berta Cáceres lost her life after preventing a dam from damaging her homeland.

3. Maria Grazia Giammarinaro
Rome, Italy
Working as a powerful judge in Rome, Maria Grazia Giammarinaro took on dangerous criminals trafficking people.

4. Althea Gibson
Jamaica
Althea Gibson won her first international tennis tournament in Jamaica in 1951.

5. Helena Gualinga
Pastaza, Ecuador
Helena Gualinga organized protests against oil companies that are damaging her country's rain forests.

6. Isra Hirsi
Minneapolis, Minnesota, United States
While still a teenager, Isra Hirsi helped set up the US Youth Climate Strike from her home base in Minneapolis.

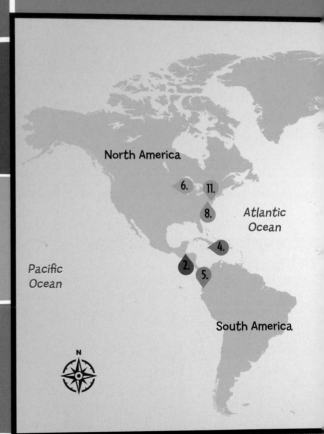

North America

Pacific Ocean

Atlantic Ocean

South America

N

7. Wangari Maathai
Nairobi, Kenya
Wangari Maathai set up the Green Belt Movement that paid women in Kenya, and then across Africa, to plant trees.

8. Michelle Obama
Washington, DC, United States

As the First Lady living in the White House in Washington, DC, Michelle Obama started promoting the rights of girls across the world to have an education.

10. Greta Thunberg
Stockholm, Sweden

Greta Thunberg went on strike in 2018. She refused to go to school and protested about climate change outside the Swedish parliament.

Arctic Ocean

10.

Europe

3.

1.

12.

Asia

Africa

9.

7.

Pacific Ocean

Indian Ocean

Australia

Southern Ocean

11. Emma Watson
New York City, New York, United States

At the United Nations headquarters in New York City, the actress Emma Watson announces a campaign to fight against gender inequality.

9. Mother Teresa
Kolkata, India

Mother Teresa cared for the sick and looked after the poorest people in the slums of Kolkata.

12. Malala Yousafzai
Mingora, Pakistan

At the age of fifteen, Malala Yousafzai was shot by an extremist in Mingora, Pakistan. She survived the attack.

Glossary

atmosphere (**at**-muhs-feer) the mixture of gases that surrounds a planet

Ayatollah (aye-oh-**toe**-luh) a religious leader in Iran

chador (**cha**-door) a loose shawl that covers the body from head to foot but leaves the face visible

chaperone (**shap**-uh-*rohn*) an adult who protects the safety of a younger person

climate change (**klye**-mit chaynj) global warming and other changes in the weather that are happening because of human activity

corruption (kuh-**ruhp**-shuhn) dishonesty and cheating by public officials

deforestation (dee-**for**-ist-ay-shun) when a large area of forested land is cleared

erosion (i-**roh**-zhuhn) the wearing away of something by water or wind

exile (**eg**-zile) a situation in which you are forbidden to live in your home country

extremists (ik-**stree**-mists) people who have extreme views, usually about religion or politics

global warming (**gloh**-buhl **warm**-ing) a rise in the temperature of Earth's atmosphere caused by humans

greenhouse gases (**green**-hous **gas**-uhs) gases such as carbon dioxide that contribute to climate change

hijab (**hi**-jab) a head covering worn in public by some Muslim women

missionary (**mish**-uh-*ner*-ee) someone who is sent to a foreign country to teach about religion and do good works

oppressive (uh-**pres**-iv) cruel

parliament (**pahr**-luh-muhnt) the group of people who have been elected to make the laws in some countries

PhD (**pee**-aitch-dee) a doctor of philosophy, a doctoral degree

poverty (**pah**-vur-tee) the state of being poor

refugees (ref-yoo-**jeez**) people who are forced to leave their home or country to escape war, religious persecution, or a natural disaster

rural (**roor**-uhl) relating to the countryside rather than to a town

slums (sluhmz) part of a city or a town where many poor people live

Swahili (swa-**hee**-lee) a language spoken in Kenya and across East Africa

Taliban (**ta**-li-ban) a brutal, extremist religious group in South Asia

Urdu (**oor**-doo) one of the languages spoken in Pakistan

Index

Further Reading

Amson-Bradshaw, Georgia. *Brilliant Women: Heroic Leaders & Activists*. New York: B.E.S. Publishing, 2018.

Jina, Devika. *The Extraordinary Life of Greta Thunberg*. New York: Puffin Books, 2020.

Swanson, Jennifer. *Environmental Activist Wangari Maathai*. Minneapolis, MN: Lerner Publications, 2018.

Yousafzai, Malala. *Malala: My Story of Standing Up for Girls' Rights*. London: Wren & Rook, 2018.

About the Author

Devra Newberger Speregen grew up in a Jewish American family in New York. Her father was a scientist, mathematician, and engineer, and her mother was a teacher and poet. Devra followed in her mother's creative footsteps and chose a career in writing. She studied theater at college, and dreamed of writing plays and musicals. But after landing her first job at Scholastic, she knew she wanted a career as an author. Devra has written more than 200 books, including a biography on Albert Einstein; and her favorite book, about her friend who is a veterinary ophthalmologist. When she's not working, Devra enjoys playing games—and hopes to invent the next big board game!

About the Consultant

Bonnie Morris grew up in California, North Carolina, and Washington, DC. She earned her PhD in women's history and is the author of nineteen books, including *Women's History For Beginners*, *The Feminist Revolution*, and *What's the Score? 25 Years of Teaching Women's Sports History*. She is also a scholarly adviser to the National Women's History Museum and a historical consultant to Disney Animation. In one of her favorite jobs as a professor, she lived on a ship and went around the world (three times!) teaching for Semester at Sea. She has kept a journal since she was twelve and has filled more than 200 notebooks using a fountain pen.